JOURNEYS

Reader's Notebook

Volume 1

Kindergarten

Houghton Mifflin Harcourt™

Volume 1
READER'S NOTEBOOK

Contents

Welcome to Kindergarten WTK1

Unit 1

Lesson 1: What Makes a Family? 1
Lesson 2: How Do Dinosaurs Go to School? 9
Lesson 3: Please, Puppy, Please 17
Lesson 4: Everybody Works 26
Lesson 5: The Handiest Things in the World 31

Unit 2

Lesson 6: My Five Senses 39
Lesson 7: Mice Squeak, We Speak 44
Lesson 8: Move! 49
Lesson 9: What Do Wheels Do All Day? 54
Lesson 10: Mouse Shapes 59

Contents

Unit 3

Name ISABEHA

Aa Bb Cc Dd Ee Ff Gg Hh Ii Jj Kk Ll Mm

Nn Oo Pp Qq Rr Ss Tt Uu Vv Ww Xx Yy Zz

M	x	A	b	S	a	F	I
r	A	a	C	a	T	n	A
O	z	L	a	A	i	A	a
a	J	a	A	h	A	A	a

Directions Have children identify and write uppercase *A* and lowercase *a*. Then have them circle all the *A*'s and *a*'s in the box.

Remind children to write the upper- and lowercase letters so they can be easily read, using a left-to-right and top-to-bottom progression.

Name _ISABELLA_

Aa Bb Cc Dd Ee Ff Gg Hh Ii Jj Kk Ll Mm

Nn Oo Pp Qq Rr Ss Tt Uu Vv Ww Xx Yy Zz

Bb Bb

B	y	B	c	T	b	G	m
s	B	b	D	b	U	o	B
P	a	M	b	B	j	B	a
S	K	b	C	i	M	B	b

Directions Have children identify and write uppercase *B* and lowercase *b*. Then have them circle all the *B*'s and *b*'s in the box.

Remind children to write the upper- and lowercase letters so they can be easily read, using a left-to-right and top-to-bottom progression.

Name _ISABELLA_

Aa Bb Cc Dd Ee Ff Gg Hh Ii Jj Kk Ll Mm

Nn Oo Pp Qq Rr Ss Tt Uu Vv Ww Xx Yy Zz

Directions Have children identify and write uppercase *C* and lowercase *c*. Then have them circle all the *C*'s and *c*'s in the box.

Remind children to write the upper- and lowercase letters so they can be easily read, using a left-to-right and top-to-bottom progression.

Letter Names

WTK 3

Kindergarten, Welcome to Kindergarten

Name ISABELLA

Aa Bb Cc Dd Ee Ff Gg Hh Ii Jj Kk Ll Mm

Nn Oo Pp Qq Rr Ss Tt Uu Vv Ww Xx Yy Zz

Dd

P	a	D	e	V	d	I	o
u	D	d	F	d	W	q	D
R	c	O	d	D	l	D	d
d	M	d	D	k	D	D	d

Directions Have children identify and write uppercase *D* and lowercase *d*. Then have them circle all the *D*'s and *d*'s in the box.

Remind children to write the upper- and lowercase letters so they can be easily read, using a left-to-right and top-to-bottom progression.

Kindergarten, Welcome to Kindergarten

Name _ISABELLA_

Aa Bb Cc Dd Ee Ff Gg Hh Ii Jj Kk Ll Mm

Nn Oo Pp Qq Rr Ss Tt Uu Vv Ww Xx Yy Zz

Ee Ee Ee Ee Ee ee ee

E	b	E	f	W	a	J	x
v	E	e	G	e	X	r	E
S	d	P	e	E	m	E	e
r	N	e	E	l	H	E	e

Directions Have children identify and write uppercase *E* and lowercase *e*. Then have them circle all the *E*'s and *e*'s in the box.

Remind children to write the upper- and lowercase letters so they can be easily read, using a left-to-right and top-to-bottom progression.

Letter Names

Kindergarten, Welcome to Kindergarten

Name _ISABELLA_

Aa Bb Cc Dd Ee Ff Gg Hh Ii Jj Kk Ll Mm

Nn Oo Pp Qq Rr Ss Tt Uu Vv Ww Xx Yy Zz

Ff

R	c	F	g	X	f	K	q
w	F	f	H	f	Y	s	F
T	e	Q	f	F	n	F	f
f	O	f	F	m	F	F	f

Directions Have children identify and write uppercase *F* and lowercase *f*. Then have them circle all the *F*'s and *f*'s in the box.

Remind children to write the upper- and lowercase letters so they can be easily read, using a left-to-right and top-to-bottom progression.

Name _____ ISABELLA _____

Aa Bb Cc Dd Ee Ff Gg Hh Ii Jj Kk Ll Mm

Nn Oo Pp Qq Rr Ss Tt Uu Vv Ww Xx Yy Zz

G g

S	d	V	h	Y	G	L	r
x	G	g	I	g	Z	t	B
U	f	R	g	G	o	G	g
b	P	g	T	s	G	G	g

Directions Have children identify and write uppercase *G* and lowercase *g*. Then have them circle all the *G*'s and *g*'s in the box.

Remind children to write the upper- and lowercase letters so they can be easily read, using a left-to-right and top-to-bottom progression.

Name _Isabella_

Aa Bb Cc Dd Ee Ff Gg Hh Ii Jj Kk Ll Mm

Nn Oo Pp Qq Rr Ss Tt Uu Vv Ww Xx Yy Zz

Hh Hh

T	e	H	i	Z	h	M	s
y	H	h	J	h	A	u	H
V	g	S	h	H	p	H	h
h	Q	h	H	o	H	H	h

Directions Have children identify and write uppercase *H* and lowercase *h*. Then have them circle all the *H*'s and *h*'s in the box.

Remind children to write the upper- and lowercase letters so they can be easily read, using a left-to-right and top-to-bottom progression.

Kindergarten, Welcome to Kindergarten

Name _ISABella_

Aa	Bb	Cc	Dd	Ee	Ff	Gg	Hh	Ii	Jj	Kk	Ll	Mm
Nn	Oo	Pp	Qq	Rr	Ss	Tt	Uu	Vv	Ww	Xx	Yy	Zz

Ii

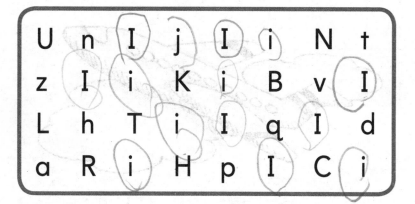

U n I j I i N t
z I i K i B v I
L h T i I q I d
a R i H p I C i

Directions Have children identify and write uppercase *I* and lowercase *i*. Then have them circle all the *I*'s and *i*'s in the box.

Remind children to write the upper- and lowercase letters so they can be easily read, using a left-to-right and top-to-bottom progression.

Name ISABGJ I A

Aa Bb Cc Dd Ee Ff Gg Hh Ii Jj Kk Ll Mm

Nn Oo Pp Qq Rr Ss Tt Uu Vv Ww Xx Yy Zz

Jj

V	g	J	k	B	j	O	u
a	J	j	L	j	C	w	J
X	i	U	j	J	r	J	j
j	S	j	J	p	J	J	j

Directions Have children identify and write uppercase *J* and lowercase *j*. Then have them circle all the *J*'s and *j*'s in the box.

Remind children to write the upper- and lowercase letters so they can be easily read, using a left-to-right and top-to-bottom progression.

Name _____

Aa Bb Cc Dd Ee Ff Gg Hh Ii Jj Kk Ll Mm

Nn Oo Pp Qq Rr Ss Tt Uu Vv Ww Xx Yy Zz

Kk

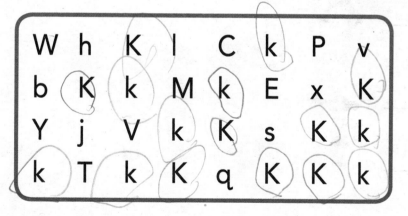

W	h	K	l	C	k	P	v
b	K	K	M	k	E	x	K
Y	j	V	k	K	s	K	k
k	T	k	K	q	K	K	k

Directions Have children identify and write uppercase *K* and lowercase *k*. Then have them circle all the *K*'s and *k*'s in the box.

Remind children to write the upper- and lowercase letters so they can be easily read, using a left-to-right and top-to-bottom progression.

Letter Names

1

Kindergarten, Unit 1

Name ISABELLA

I

1. Jump .

2. Run .

3. DrinK .

Directions Have children look at each picture and name the action. Then have them write the word *I* to complete each sentence. Have children read the completed sentences aloud.

Have children tap their desks once for each word as they read the sentences aloud again. Have children say other sentences with the word *I*.

Words to Know

Kindergarten, Unit 1

Name _____

Aa Bb Cc Dd Ee Ff Gg Hh Ii Jj Kk Ll Mm

Nn Oo Pp Qq Rr Ss Tt Uu Vv Ww Xx Yy Zz

Directions Have children identify and write uppercase *L* and lowercase *l*. Then have them circle all the *L*'s and *l*'s in the box.

Remind children to write the upper- and lowercase letters so they can be easily read, using a left-to-right and top-to-bottom progression.

Letter Names

3

Kindergarten, Unit 1

Name _Issy_

Aa Bb Cc Dd Ee Ff Gg Hh Ii Jj Kk Ll Mm

Nn Oo Pp Qq Rr Ss Tt Uu Vv Ww Xx Yy Zz

Mm   Mm

Y	j	B	n	M	m	R	x
d	M	m	O	m	G	z	L
A	l	X	m	M	u	D	m
g	V	m	M	s	e	M	m

Directions Have children identify and write uppercase *M* and lowercase *m*. Then have them circle all the *M*'s and *m*'s in the box.

Remind children to write the upper- and lowercase letters so they can be easily read, using a left-to-right and top-to-bottom progression.

4

Name _____

Main Ideas

Directions Tell children to draw a picture to show some important facts they learned about families from the Big Book. Have children share their pictures with the class. Tell them to speak clearly and use complete sentences as they share information.

In addition, tell them to listen carefully as others speak and to face others as they share.

Comprehension

5

Kindergarten, Unit 1

Name _____

Aa Bb Cc Dd Ee Ff Gg Hh Ii Jj Kk Ll Mm

Nn Oo Pp Qq Rr Ss Tt Uu Vv Ww Xx Yy Zz

N n

Z	k	N	O	F	n	S	y
e	N	n	P	n	H	a	N
B	m	Y	n	N	v	N	n
n	W	n	N	t	N	N	n

Directions Have children identify and write uppercase *N* and lowercase *n*. Then have them circle all the *N*'s and *n*'s in the box.

Remind children to write the upper- and lowercase letters so they can be easily read, using a left-to-right and top-to-bottom progression.

Letter Names

Kindergarten, Unit 1

Name _ISABELLA_

Aa Bb Cc Dd Ee Ff Gg Hh Ii Jj Kk Ll Mm

Nn Oo Pp Qq Rr Ss Tt Uu Vv Ww Xx Yy Zz

Oo

A	l	H	o	G	p	T	z
d	O	o	Q	h	I	b	T
C	n	Z	o	O	w	O	o
o	X	o	O	u	A	O	b

Directions Have children identify and write uppercase *O* and lowercase *o*. Then have them circle all the *O*'s and *o*'s in the box.

Remind children to write the upper- and lowercase letters so they can be easily read, using a left-to-right and top-to-bottom progression.

Letter Names

7

Kindergarten, Unit 1

Name _Issy_

Nouns for People

1.

2.

3.

Directions Have children look at the first row of pictures and underline the mother. Have them look at the second row and underline the father. Then have them look at the third row and underline the grandmother. Then have children identify the pictures of the grown-ups in each row and draw a circle around them. Tell children to draw a picture in the box of someone in their family. Have them label their picture and then tell about it.

8

Name _____

Aa Bb Cc Dd Ee Ff Gg Hh Ii Jj Kk Ll Mm

Nn Oo Pp Qq Rr Ss Tt Uu Vv Ww Xx Yy Zz

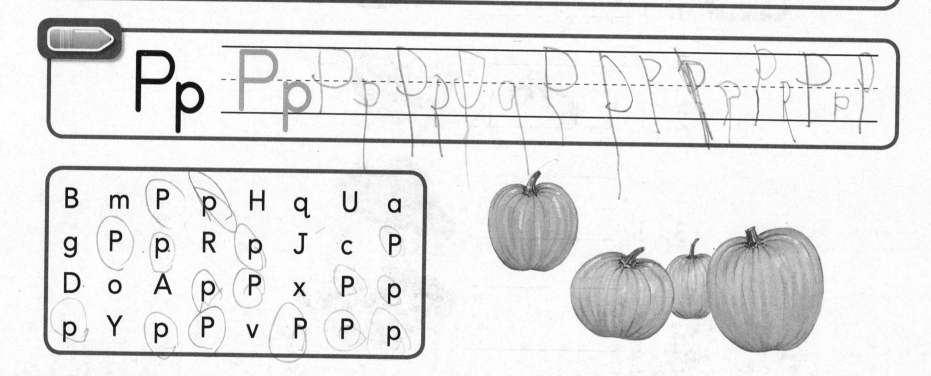

Pp

B	m	P	p	H	q	U	a
g	P	p	R	p	J	c	P
D	o	A	p	P	x	P	p
p	Y	p	P	v	P	P	p

Directions Have children identify and write uppercase *P* and lowercase *p*. Then have them circle all the *P*'s and *p*'s in the box.

Remind children to write the upper- and lowercase letters so they can be easily read, using a left-to-right and top-to-bottom progression.

Letter Names

9

Kindergarten, Unit 1

Lesson 2
READER'S NOTEBOOK

How Do Dinosaurs Go to School?
Words to Know: like

Name

like

1. I _like_

2. I _like_

3. I _like_

4. I _like_

Directions Have children read the word *I* and name each picture. Then have them write the word *like* to complete each sentence. Have children read the completed sentences aloud.

Have children point to and say the names of letters they recognize on the page. Then have children tap their desks once for each word as they read the sentences aloud again. Have children say other sentences with the word *like*.

Words to Know

Kindergarten, Unit 1

Name ISABELLA

Aa Bb Cc Dd Ee Ff Gg Hh Ii Jj Kk Ll Mm

Nn Oo Pp Qq Rr Ss Tt Uu Vv Ww Xx Yy Zz

Qq Qq

C	n	Q	q	I	r	V	b
Q	Q	q	S	q	K	d	Q
E	p	B	q	Q	y	K	s
q	Z	m	Q	w	J	Q	q

Directions Have children identify and write uppercase *Q* and lowercase *q*. Then have them circle all the *Q*'s and *q*'s in the box.

Remind children to write the upper- and lowercase letters so they can be easily read, using a left-to-right and top-to-bottom progression.

Letter Names

11

Kindergarten, Unit 1

Name ___ISABELLA___

Aa Bb Cc Dd Ee Ff Gg Hh Ii Jj Kk Ll Mm

Nn Oo Pp Qq Rr Ss Tt Uu Vv Ww Xx Yy Zz

Rr

D	o	R	r	J	s	W	c
i	R	r	T	r	L	e	R
F	q	C	r	R	z	R	r
r	A	r	R	x	R	R	r

Directions Have children identify and write uppercase *R* and lowercase *r*. Then have them circle all the *R*'s and *r*'s in the box.

Remind children to write the upper- and lowercase letters so they can be easily read, using a left-to-right and top-to-bottom progression.

Letter Names

Kindergarten, Unit 1

Name ___Issy___

Understanding Characters

Directions Tell children to draw a picture that shows how their favorite character feels in the story. Then have them draw a picture to show how they would feel if they were in a classroom with a dinosaur. Have children share their pictures and talk about both. Tell them to speak clearly and use complete sentences as they share their ideas about the characters with classmates.

Name _Isabella_

Aa Bb Cc Dd Ee Ff Gg Hh Ii Jj Kk Ll Mm

Nn Oo Pp Qq Rr Ss Tt Uu Vv Ww Xx Yy Zz

Ss S s

E	p	S	s	K	t	s	d
j	S	s	U	G	M	f	S
G	r	D	s	S	a	S	o
h	B	s	Q	y	S	S	s

Directions Have children identify and write uppercase *S* and lowercase *s*. Then have them circle all the *S*'s and *s*'s in the box.

Remind children to write the upper- and lowercase letters so they can be easily read, using a left-to-right and top-to-bottom progression.

Letter Names

Kindergarten, Unit 1

Name _Isabella_

Aa Bb Cc Dd Ee Ff Gg Hh Ii Jj Kk Ll Mm

Nn Oo Pp Qq Rr Ss Tt Uu Vv Ww Xx Yy Zz

Tt T Tt T T T T T T T T

F q T t L u Y e
j T t V t N g T
H s E t T b T t
t C t T z T T t

Directions Have children identify and write uppercase *T* and lowercase *t*. Then have them circle all the *T*'s and *t*'s in the box.

Remind children to write the upper- and lowercase letters so they can be easily read, using a left-to-right and top-to-bottom progression.

Letter Names

15

Kindergarten, Unit 1

Name _____

Nouns for Places

1.

2. (house) (dinosaur)

3.

Directions Have children name the pictures in the first row. Have them underline the picture that shows a place. Repeat for the second and third rows.

Then have children draw a picture of a favorite place in the box. Have them label their picture and then tell about it.

Grammar

16

Kindergarten, Unit 1

Name _____ *ISABELLA*

Aa Bb Cc Dd Ee Ff Gg Hh Ii Jj Kk Ll Mm

Nn Oo Pp Qq Rr Ss Tt Uu Vv Ww Xx Yy Zz

Uu _____

G r U r M v Z f
k U u W p O h U
I t F u U c U d
A D u B a U Y u

Directions Have children identify and write uppercase *U* and lowercase *u*. Then have them circle all the *U*'s and *u*'s in the box.

Remind children to write the upper- and lowercase letters so they can be easily read, using a left-to-right and top-to-bottom progression.

Letter Names

17

Kindergarten, Unit 1

Name _ISABELLA_

the

1. I like _THE_ .

2. I like _THE_ .

3. I like _THE_ .

Directions Have children read the words *I like* and name each picture. Then have them write the word *the* to complete each sentence. Have children read the completed sentences aloud.

Have children point to and say the names of letters they recognize on the page. Then have children tap their desks once for each word as they read the sentences aloud again. Have children say other sentences with the word *the*.

18

Name _ISABELA_

Aa Bb Cc Dd Ee Ff Gg Hh Ii Jj Kk Ll Mm

Nn Oo Pp Qq Rr Ss Tt Uu Vv Ww Xx Yy Zz

Vv

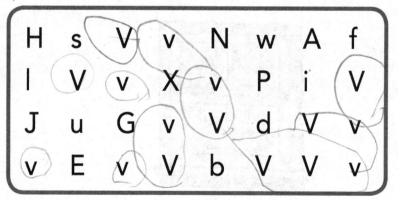

H s V v N w A f
I V v X v P i V
J u G v V d V v
v E v V b V V v

Directions Have children identify and write uppercase *V* and lowercase *v*. Then have them circle all the *V*'s and *v*'s in the box.

Remind children to write the upper- and lowercase letters so they can be easily read, using a left-to-right and top-to-bottom progression.

Name _____ *ISABC IIA*

Name _____ *ISABC IIA*

Aa Bb Cc Dd Ee Ff Gg Hh Ii Jj Kk Ll Mm

Nn Oo Pp Qq Rr Ss Tt Uu Vv Ww Xx Yy Zz

Ww   W w

Directions Have children identify and write uppercase *W* and lowercase *w*. Then have them circle all the *W*'s and *w*'s in the box.

Remind children to write the upper- and lowercase letters so they can be easily read, using a left-to-right and top-to-bottom progression.

20

Letter Names
© Houghton Mifflin Harcourt Publishing Company. All rights reserved.

Kindergarten, Unit 1

Name ISAB Chia

Story Structure

Directions Tell children to draw a picture of the main character in the story. Have them also show the setting in the background. Then have them draw a picture to show their favorite event in the story. Have children share their pictures and describe their drawings. Then have them retell or act out the key event they illustrated.

Comprehension

21

Kindergarten, Unit 1

Name _ISA BELLA_

Aa Bb Cc Dd Ee Ff Gg Hh Ii Jj Kk Ll Mm

Nn Oo Pp Qq Rr Ss Tt Uu Vv Ww Xx Yy Zz

Xx

J u X x P y C h
n X x Z x R k X
L w I x X f X x
x G x X d X X x

Directions Have children identify and write uppercase *X* and lowercase *x*. Then have them circle all the *X*'s and *x*'s in the box.

Remind children to write the upper- and lowercase letters so they can be easily read, using a left-to-right and top-to-bottom progression.

22

Letter Names
© Houghton Mifflin Harcourt Publishing Company. All rights reserved.

Kindergarten, Unit 1

Name **Issy**

Aa Bb Cc Dd Ee Ff Gg Hh Ii Jj Kk Ll Mm

Nn Oo Pp Qq Rr Ss Tt Uu Vv Ww Xx Yy Zz

Yy

K	v	G	y	Q	z	D	i
o	E	y	A	y	S	l	Y
M	x	J	y	Y	y	Y	y
n	H	y	F	e	Y	Z	D

Directions Have children identify and write uppercase *Y* and lowercase *y*. Then have them circle all the *Y*'s and *y*'s in the box.

Remind children to write the upper- and lowercase letters so they can be easily read, using a left-to-right and top-to-bottom progression.

Name _ISAy IIA_

Aa Bb Cc Dd Ee Ff Gg Hh Ii Jj Kk Ll Mm

Nn Oo Pp Qq Rr Ss Tt Uu Vv Ww Xx Yy Zz

L	w	Z	z	R	a	E	j
p	Z	z	B	z	T	m	Z
N	y	K	z	Z	h	Z	z
z	I	z	Z	f	Z	Z	z

Directions Have children identify and write uppercase *Z* and lowercase *z*. Then have them circle all the *Z*'s and *z*'s in the box.

Remind children to write the upper- and lowercase letters so they can be easily read, using a left-to-right and top-to-bottom progression.

Kindergarten, Unit 1

Nouns for Animals and Things

Vampire

Directions Have children name the pictures in the first row. Have them tell whether each picture shows an animal or a thing. Have them underline the picture that shows an animal and draw a circle around the picture that shows a thing.

Repeat for the second and third rows. Then have children draw a picture in the box of a favorite animal or thing. Have them dictate or write a caption for their picture.

Grammar

25

Kindergarten, Unit 1

Name ISABELLA

and

1. I like And .

2. I like And .

3. I like And .

4. I like And .

Directions Have children read the words *I like* and name each picture. Then have them write the word *and* to complete each sentence. Have children read the completed sentences aloud.

Have children point to and say the names of letters they recognize on the page. Then have children tap their desks once for each word as they read the sentences aloud again. Have children say other sentences with the word *and*.

Name _ISABELA_

1. m Mm Mm   M   M

2.

 T

 D

 M

 C

 M

 M

Directions Have children name the Alphafriend and its letter. Have them trace and write *M* and *m*. Then name the pictures (*monkey, mittens, truck, man, motorcycle, mug, milk, moose*) and have children write *Mm* next to the pictures whose names start with the /m/ sound. Help children think of groups of words that begin with the /m/ sound. For example, *My monkey moves more*.

27

Name

1.

2.

Directions Have children name the Alphafriend and its letter. Have them trace and write *Mm*. Remind children to write the upper- and lowercase letters so they can be easily read, using a left-to-right and top-to-bottom progression. Then tell children to name each picture (*chair, mask, mat, monkey, teapot, marble*) and write the letter *m* when they hear the /m/ sound at the beginning of a word.

Phonics

28

Kindergarten, Unit 1

Name _____ ISSY _____

Text and Graphic Features

1.

2.

Directions Tell children to look at the first set of pictures. Have them circle the picture that best shows a man who helps children cross the street. Have children identify the sign and explain why the man is holding it. Then have them look at the second set of pictures and circle the picture that best shows a girl who delivers newspapers. Discuss with children how they matched your spoken words to the correct picture. Then ask children how pictures can help them better understand information in a text.

Comprehension

Kindergarten, Unit 1

Name _____

Action Verbs in the Present Tense

| I   like |

1. I _____

2. _____

Directions Have children name each picture. Then have them complete each sentence by writing a word from the box and circling the picture that shows an action. Have children identify and act out each of the action words. Have children read their sentences aloud using an action word to describe the picture they circled. Tell them to speak clearly as they share their sentences and to listen carefully to others as they share.

Grammar

30

Kindergarten, Unit 1

Name _____

$$\boxed{\text{I} \quad \text{like} \quad \text{the} \quad \text{and}}$$

 1. I _____ the .

2. I like _____ .

3. _____ like the .

 4. I like _____ .

Directions Have children read the words in the box and name each picture. Then have them write the correct word from the box to complete each sentence. Have children read the completed sentences aloud.

Have children point to and say the names of the letters they recognize on the page. Then have them read the sentences aloud again and tap their desks once for each word. Have children tell a story using all of the Words to Know.

Words to Know

Kindergarten, Unit 1

Name _____

My Story

Directions Help children **generate ideas** for their own story. Have children write ideas and draw pictures in the space provided in the idea web. Guide children to write words or draw pictures showing the characters, setting, and what will happen in their stories.

Writing

Kindergarten, Unit 1

Name _____

1. **S** s

2.

Directions Have children name the Alphafriend and its letter. Have them trace and write *Ss*. Then have them write *Ss* next to the pictures whose names start with the /s/ sound.

Help children think of groups of words that begin with the /s/ sound. For example, *Sarah says six sentences.*

Name _____

My Story

Directions Have children use pages 34–35 to draft, revise and edit a story. Encourage children to use their ideas from **Reader's Notebook** page 32 as a guide in their writing. As children **develop their drafts,** remind them that they will have a chance to add to their story on another day. Remind children to include events for the beginning, middle, and end of their story. As children **revise their drafts,** discuss sentences and details they could add to make their story even better. Remind children to include a sentence at the end that tells about their reaction to the story. As children **edit their drafts,** help them use what they know about letters and sounds to check the spelling of words. Have them check spelling using other sources as appropriate. Have children also check their sentences for correct capitalization and punctuation.

Name _____

My Story

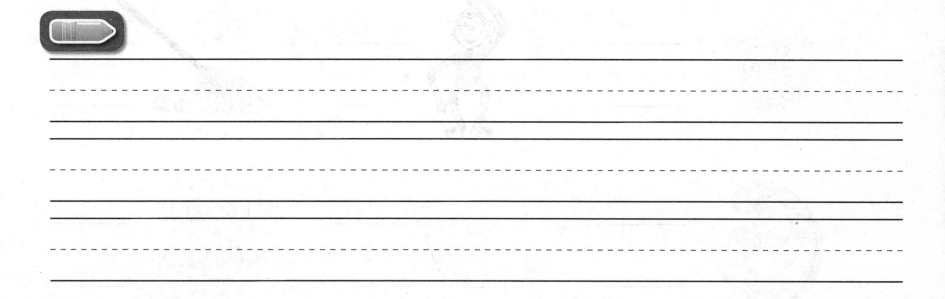

Directions Have children use pages 34–35 to draft, revise and edit a story. Encourage children to use their ideas from **Reader's Notebook** page 32 as a guide in their writing. As children **develop their drafts,** remind them that they will have a chance to add to their story on another day. Remind children to include events for the beginning, middle, and end of their story. As children **revise their drafts,** discuss sentences and details they could add to make their story even better. Remind children to include a sentence at the end that tells about their reaction to the story. As children **edit their drafts,** help them use what they know about letters and sounds to check the spelling of words. Have them check spelling using other sources as appropriate. Have children also check their sentences for correct capitalization and punctuation.

Writing

Kindergarten, Unit 1

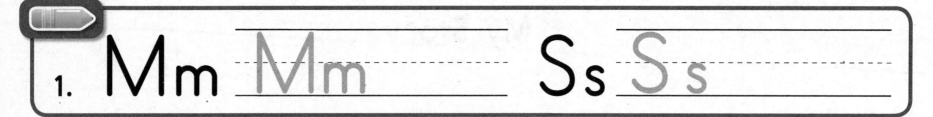

1. Mm Mm   Ss Ss

2.

Directions Have children name each letter. Have them write
Mm and *Ss*. Then tell children to name the pictures and write
the letter for the sound they hear at the beginning of each
picture name.

Remind children to write the upper- and lowercase letters so
they can be easily read, using a left-to-right and top-to-bottom
progression.

Phonics
© Houghton Mifflin Harcourt Publishing Company. All rights reserved.

36

Kindergarten, Unit 1

Name _____

Details

Directions Have children draw one of the handy tools from the **Big Book.** Have them share their pictures with a group. Have children explain how the tool makes a job or activity easier.

Remind them to speak clearly and use complete sentences as they describe the tools and how they help people do things.

Name _____

Action Verbs in the Present Tense

I   like

1. I _____

2. _____ like

Directions Have children name each picture. Have them complete each sentence by writing a word from the box and circling the picture that shows an action.

Have children read their sentences aloud using an action word to describe the picture they circled. Tell them to speak clearly as they share their sentences and to listen carefully to others as they share.

Grammar

38

Kindergarten, Unit 1

Name _____

$$\boxed{\textbf{see}}$$

 1. I _____ the .

2. I _____ the ⬭ .

3. I _____ the .

Directions Have children read the word in the box and name each picture. Then have them write the word *see* to complete each sentence. Have children read the completed sentences aloud.

Have children point to and say the names of letters they recognize on the page. Then have children tap their desks once for each word as they read the sentences aloud again. Have children say other sentences with the word *see*.

Words to Know

39

Kindergarten, Unit 2

Name _____

1. Aa Aa _____ _____

2.

 _____

 _____

_____

 _____

 _____

 _____

 _____

Phonics

Kindergarten, Unit 2

Name _____

1. _____ _____

2.

Directions Have children write their name at the top of the page. Have them trace and write *Aa* and *Mm*. Then help children name the pictures (*monkey, ax, alligator, motorbike, mittens,* *ambulance*) and write the capital and lowercase letters that stand for the sound they hear at the beginning of each name. Remind children to write the upper- and lowercase letters so they can be easily read, using a left-to-right and top-to-bottom progression.

Phonics

41

Kindergarten, Unit 2

Compare and Contrast

 1. I can taste the .

3.

2. I can touch the .

Directions Read the sentences aloud with children and discuss how our senses are alike and different. Have children draw pictures to show themselves tasting ice cream or touching a bunny. Have them write one-word captions. Have children identify the sense they chose and sort their pictures (taste or touch). Discuss the pictures in each category. Then reread pages 3–10 of the Big Book. Have children pantomime the actions in the pictures.

Comprehension

Kindergarten, Unit 2

Name _____

Sensory Words

Directions Tell children to look at and name the pictures. Have children draw a line from each sense in the top row to the picture it describes in the bottom row. Have children write a complete sentence that describes one of the pictures. Have them include sensory words in their sentences. Have them share their sentences with the class.

Grammar

Kindergarten, Unit 2

Name _____

We

1. _____ see the .

2. _____ see the 🐱 .

3. _____ see the 🐱 and 🚗 .

Directions Have children write their name at the top of the page. Have children read the word in the box and name each picture. Then have them write the word *We* to complete each sentence. Have children read the completed sentences aloud.

Have children point to and say the names of letters they recognize on the page. Then have children tap their desks once for each word as they read the sentences aloud again. Have children say other sentences with the word *we*.

44

Name _____

1.

2.

Directions Have children write their name at the top of the page. Have children trace and write *T* and *t*. Then help them name the pictures (*towel, tent, toaster, table, window, tea, ladder, telephone*). Have children write *Tt* next to the pictures whose names start with the /t/ sound.
Help children think of groups of words that begin with the /t/ sound. For example, *tiger, touchdown, trumpet, taste.*

Name _____

1. Aa _Aa_____ Tt _Tt_____

2.

  _____

  _____

  _____

  _____

  _____

  _____

Directions Have children name, trace, and write *Aa* and *Tt*. Then help children name the pictures (*tent, apple, ants, ten, table, alligator*) and write the capital and lowercase letters that stand for the sound they hear at the beginning of each picture name.

Remind children to write the upper- and lowercase letters so they can be easily read, using a left-to-right and top-to-bottom progression.

46

Phonics

Kindergarten, Unit 2

Name _____

Understanding Characters

Directions Tell children to draw a picture of their favorite animal character from *Mice Squeak, We Speak*. Then have them draw a picture to show how they think the animal feels when it makes its sound.

Have children share their pictures. Page through the Big Book and have children identify each character.

Comprehension

47

Kindergarten, Unit 2

Name _____

Sensory Words

Directions Have children name the pictures in each row. Have them draw a line from each sense in the top row to the picture it describes in the bottom row. Then have children write a complete sentence that describes one of the pictures.

Have them include sensory words in their sentences. Ask children to share their sentences with the class.

Grammar

Kindergarten, Unit 2

Name _____

a

1. I like _____ .

2. I like _____ .

3. We like _____ .

Directions Have children write their name at the top of the page. Then have them read the word in the box, name each rebus picture (*cat, dog, fish tank*), and write the word *a* to complete each sentence. Have children read the completed sentences aloud.

Have children point to and say the names of letters they recognize on the page. Then have them tap their desks once for each word as they read the sentences aloud again. Have children say other sentences with the word *a*.

Words to Know

49

Kindergarten, Unit 2

Name _____

1. Cc _____ _____ carrot _____

2.

 _____

_____ baseball _____

 _____

cup _____

cake _____

fence _____

Directions Have children write their name at the top of the page. Have them name the Alphafriend and its letter and trace and write C and c. Then name the pictures together (*cat, carrot, cow, ball, camera, cup, cake, gate*) and have children write Cc next to the pictures whose names start with the /k/ sound. Help children think of groups of words that begin with the /k/ sound, for example, *cart, cupcake, cap*.

Phonics

Kindergarten, Unit 2

1. A a   A a   C c   C c

2.

 _____

 _____

 _____

 _____

 _____

 _____

Directions Have children write their name at the top of the page. Then have them name and write *Aa* and *Cc*. Name the pictures together (*alligator, candle, cup, axe, ants, camera*) and ask children to write the capital and lowercase letters for the sound they hear at the beginning of each picture name.

Remind children to write the upper- and lowercase letters so they can be easily read, using a left-to-right and top-to-bottom progression.

Name _____

Details

Directions Tell children to draw a picture of one of the animals in the Big Book. Have them share their pictures with the class. Have children use describing words to tell what the animal looks like and how it moves.

Remind them to speak clearly and use complete sentences as they describe their pictures. Then have children tell which words are describing words.

Comprehension

Kindergarten, Unit 2

Name _____

Adjectives for Color

| purple   red   brown |

1. Look at the _____ wagon.

2. I have a pair of _____ mittens.

3. It is a _____ coat.

4. _____

Name _____

1. I like _____ .

2. I like _____ .

3. We like _____ .

Have children read the word in the box and name each picture. Then have them write the word *to* to complete each sentence. Have children read the completed sentences aloud.

Have children point to and say the names of letters they recognize on the page. Then have children tap their desks once for each word as they read the sentences aloud again. Have children say other sentences with the word *to*.

54

Kindergarten, Unit 2

Name _____

 1. P p P p _____ _____ _____

2.

 _____   _____   _____

 _____   _____   _____

Directions Have children name the Alphafriend and its letter. Have them trace and write *P* and *p*. Then name the pictures together (*pail, pumpkin, chair, pillow, paintbrush, penny, wagon, pie*).

Have children write *Pp* next to the pictures whose names start with the /p/ sound.

Help children think of groups of words that begin with the /p/ sound, for example, *puppy, pillow, package*.

Phonics

55

Kindergarten, Unit 2

Name _____

1.

2.

 _____

 _____

 _____

 _____

 _____

 _____

Directions Have children name each letter. Have them trace and write *Tt* and *Pp*. Then help children name the pictures (*tomatoes, pumpkin, pail, table, towel, paintbrush*). Have children write the capital and lowercase letters for the sound they hear at the beginning of each name.

Remind children to write the upper- and lowercase letters so they can be easily read, using a left-to-right and top-to-bottom progression.

Text and Graphic Features

1.

2.

Directions Tell children to look at the first row of pictures. Have them circle the picture that best shows wheels helping people to win a race. Then have them look at the second row of pictures and circle the picture that best shows wheels helping people get from place to place. Discuss with children how pictures can help them better understand information they read about. Then have children use action words, such as *roll, whiz, spin,* to describe how wheels move. Have them name the action words.

Comprehension

57

Kindergarten, Unit 2

Name _____

Adjectives for Numbers

| seven   two   five |

1. The bike has _____ wheels.

2. The _____ ducks swim.

3. There are _____ hats.

4. _____

Directions Discuss the pictures with children and read each sentence frame aloud. Have children complete each sentence frame by writing a word from the box on the line.

Then have children write a complete sentence using one of the number words. Have them share their sentences with the class.

Name _____

| see | we | a | to |

1. I _____ a .

2. I see _____ .

3. _____ see a .

4. We like _____ .

Directions Remind children to write their names. Have children read the words in the box and name each picture. Then have them write the word *see, we, a,* or *to* to complete each sentence. Guide children to capitalize *we* at the beginning of the third sentence. Have children read the completed sentences aloud. Then have children tell a story about the page, using all of the Words to Know.

Name _____

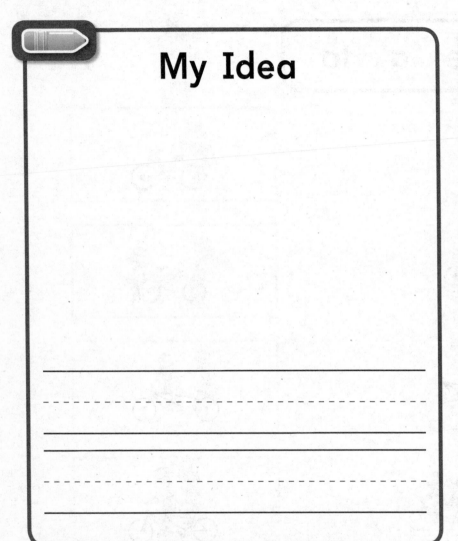

My Idea

My Idea

Directions Help children **generate ideas** for their own informative descriptions.

Guide children to draw pictures of the things they are thinking of writing about. Then have children write words that describe each idea. Remind them to include details about size and shape.

Name _____

1. Aa Aa Cc Cc Tt Tt Pp Pp

2.

 _____

 _____

 _____

 _____

 _____

 _____

Directions Remind children to write their names at the top. Then have children name each letter in row 1. Have them trace *Aa, Cc, Tt,* and *Pp*. Then tell children to name the pictures (*pumpkin, cow, towel, alligator, axe, ten*) and write the capital and lowercase letters for the sound they hear at the beginning of each picture name.

Remind children to write the upper- and lowercase letters so they can be easily read, using a left-to-right and top-to-bottom progression.

Phonics

Kindergarten, Unit 2

61

Name

My Description

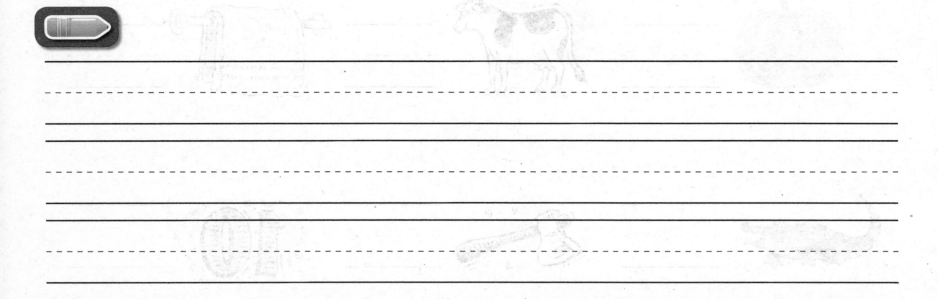

Directions Have children use pages 62–63 to draft, revise, and edit an informative description. Encourage children to use their ideas from **Reader's Notebook** page 60 as a guide in their writing. As children **develop their drafts**, remind them that they will have a chance to add to their description on another day. As children **revise their drafts**, discuss sentences and details they could add to make their description even better. For example, could they add some more shape and size adjectives? As children **edit their drafts**, help them use what they know about letters and sounds to check the spelling of words. Have them check spelling, using other sources as appropriate. Have children also check their sentences for correct capitalization and punctuation.

Name _____

My Description

Directions Have children use pages 62–63 to draft, revise, and edit an informative description. Encourage children to use their ideas from **Reader's Notebook** page 60 as a guide in their writing. As children **develop their drafts**, remind them that they will have a chance to add to their description on another day. As children **revise their drafts**, discuss sentences and details they could add to make their description even better. For example, could they add some more shape and size adjectives? As children **edit their drafts**, help them use what they know about letters and sounds to check the spelling of words. Have them check spelling, using other sources as appropriate. Have children also check their sentences for correct capitalization and punctuation.

Writing

Kindergarten, Unit 2

1. A a A a C c C c T t T t P p P p

2.

 _____

 _____

 _____

 _____

 _____

 _____

Directions Remind children to write their names. Then have children name each letter in row 1. Have them trace *Aa, Cc, Tt,* and *Pp*. Then help children name the pictures (*peanuts, cone, teeth, ambulance, cane, pajamas*) and write the capital and lowercase letters for the sound they hear at the beginning of each picture name. Remind children to write the upper- and lowercase letters so they can be easily read, using a left-to-right and top-to-bottom progression.

Name _____

Story Structure

Directions Discuss with children who the Big Book story is about and where it takes place. Then have them draw a picture of something that happens at the beginning of the story and at the end of the story. Have children share their pictures.

Have them use location words, such as *above, below,* or *next to* to describe parts of their pictures. Then have children sort the shapes at the top of the page into categories. Have them color the circles red, the squares yellow, and the triangles blue.

Comprehension

65

Kindergarten, Unit 2

Name _____

Adjectives for Size and Shape

round long small

1. My dog has _____ ears.

2. We sit on a _____ rug.

3. The _____ mouse eats cheese.

4. _____

Directions Discuss the pictures with children and read each sentence frame aloud. Have children complete each sentence frame by writing a word from the box on the line. Have them circle the word that tells about shape and underline the words that tell about size. Then have children write a complete sentence using one of the size or shape words. Have them share their sentences with the class.

Grammar

66

Kindergarten, Unit 2

Name _____

---

come   me

---

1. I see Sam.

_____

2. Come to _____, Sam.

_____

3. _____ to me, Sam.

_____

4. See Sam _____!

Directions Have children read the words in the box and look at each picture. Then have them write the word *come* or *me* to complete each sentence. Guide children to capitalize *come* at the beginning of the third sentence. Then have children read the sentences aloud. Have children point to and say the names of letters they recognize on the page. Then have children identify the action verb. Have children say other sentences with the words *come* and *me*.

Words to Know

Kindergarten, Unit 3

Name _____

1. A a   A a

2.

   _____

   _____

   _____

   _____

   _____

   _____

Directions Have children write their name at the top of the page. Have them name the Alphafriend and its letter. Then have children write *Aa*. Next help children identify the pictures.

Tell children to name each picture and write the letters *Aa* when they hear the short *a* sound somewhere in the word. Remind children to write the upper- and lowercase letters so they can be easily read, using a left-to-right and top-to-bottom progression.

Name _____

Words with *a*

 1.

cap   sat

2.

mat   Pam

3.

tap   cat

4.

mat   pat

Directions Tell children to look at the first picture. Then have them circle the word that matches the picture. Repeat with the rest of the pictures and words.

Have children say the words that match each picture. Then have them think of words that rhyme with each one.

Phonics

69

Kindergarten, Unit 3

Name _____

Compare and Contrast

1. I can .   3.

2. I can

Directions Read the sentences aloud with children and discuss how the two pictures are alike and different. Then have children draw a picture to show something they like to do in the summer or winter. Have them share their pictures.

Ask them to say where their pictures take place and use location words, such as *above* or *below*, to describe parts of their pictures.

Comprehension

Kindergarten, Unit 3

Sentence Parts: Subject

1. The dog chews a bone.

2. Sara sleeps.

3. The children like to slide.

4. _____

Directions Discuss the pictures with children and read each sentence aloud. Have children underline the naming part, or subject, in each sentence.

Then have children write a complete sentence. Have them share their sentences with the class. Challenge the class to identify the subject in each sentence.

Name _____

with   my

1. See _____ cat.

2. See my cat _____ a can.

3. See my cat _____ a mat.

4. See _____ cat.

Directions Have children read the words in the box and look at each picture. Then have them write the word *with* or *my* to complete each sentence. Have children read the completed sentences aloud.

Have children point to and say the names of the letters they recognize on the page. Then have children tap their desks once for each word as they read the sentences aloud again. Have children say other sentences with the words *with* and *my*.

Words to Know

Kindergarten, Unit 3

Name _____

1.

2.

Directions Have children write their name at the top of the page. Have them name the Alphafriend and its letter. Then have children trace and write *N* and *n*. Next, help children identify the pictures.

Have children write *Nn* next to the pictures whose names start with the /n/ sound. Help children think of groups of words that begin with the /n/ sound, for example, *Nan knits nightly*.

Phonics

73

Words with *n*

1.

_____
- - - - - - -
_____ **a n**

2.

_____
- - - - - - -
_____ **a p**

3.

m a _____
- - - - - - -

4.

_____
- - - - - - -
c _____ **n**

Directions Tell children to look at the first picture and help them name it. Then have them write the missing letter to complete the picture's name. Repeat with the rest of the pictures and words.

Say pairs of rhyming and non-rhyming words that go with each picture. Have children raise their hand when they hear a pair of words that rhyme.

Phonics

Kindergarten, Unit 3

Name _____

Conclusions

Directions Have children look at the pictures and remind them what happened at the beginning of the story. Then have children illustrate how the bear feels when he hears the snow is coming. Have children share their pictures with the class.

Discuss with children how they used what they already knew and what they learned from the story when they drew their pictures.

Comprehension

Kindergarten, Unit 3

Name _____

Sentence Parts: Verb

1. The mouse rides a bike.

2. Josh builds a snowman.

3. The cat naps.

4. _____

Name _____

you   what

1. _____ come with me.

2. _____ can we see?

3. We can see _____ and me!

Directions Have children read the words in the box and look at each picture. Then have them write the word *you* or *what* to complete each sentence. Guide children to capitalize the first letter at the beginning of a sentence. Then have children read the sentences aloud. Have children point to and say the names of the letters they recognize on the page. Then have children clap once for each word as they read the sentences aloud again. Have children say other sentences with the words *you* and *what*.

Words to Know

Kindergarten, Unit 3

Name _____

1.

2.

Directions Have children write their name at the top of the
page. Have them name the Alphafriend and its letter. Then have
children trace and write *F* and *f*.

Next, help children identify the pictures. Have children write *Ff*
next to the pictures whose names begin with the /f/ sound. Help
children think of groups of words that begin with the /f/ sound,
for example, *Four frogs fell far.*

Phonics
© Houghton Mifflin Harcourt Publishing Company. All rights reserved.

78

Kindergarten, Unit 3

Name _____

Words with *f*

 1.

fan   **can**

2.

man   **fan**

3.

fat   **pan**

4.

fat   **cap**

Directions Tell children to look at the first picture. Then have them circle the word that matches the picture. Repeat with the rest of the pictures and words.

Have children say the words that match each picture. Then have them think of words that rhyme with each one.

79

Phonics

Name _____

Author's Purpose

_____   _____   _____

_____   _____   _____

Directions Tell children to look at the pictures in the boxes and identify each one. Read the following sentence starter aloud and model how to complete it for box 1: *The author wanted me to know about___*. Have children do their best to write the response below the first box. Repeat for each remaining box. Then have children circle the animals for which the same body part was featured.

Comprehension

80

Kindergarten, Unit 3

Name _____

Complete Sentences

 1. we see a red rose

2. the brown dog

3. _____

4. _____

Directions Read aloud the page with children. Have children circle the happy face if the words are a complete sentence and the sad face if they are not. Then help children make each sentence complete. As children rewrite each sentence, have them capitalize the first letter in the sentence and put a period at the end.

Name _____

are   now

1. _____ you Sam?

2. You _____ Nat.

3. _____ you Sam?

4. _____ I see you, Sam!

Directions Have children read the words in the box and look at each picture. Then have them write the word *are* or *now* to complete each sentence. Guide children to capitalize the first letter at the beginning of a sentence. Then have children read the senten- ces aloud. Have children point to and say the names of the letters they recognize on the page. Then have children tap their desks once for each word as they read the sentences aloud again. Have children say other sentences with the words *are* and *now*.

82

Words to Know

Name _____

1.

2.

Directions Have children write their name at the top of the page. Have them name the Alphafriend and its letter. Then have children trace and write *B* and *b*. Next, help children identify the pictures.

Have children write *Bb* next to the pictures whose names begin with the /b/ sound. Help children think of groups of words that begin with the /b/ sound, for example, *Busy blue birds blink.*

Name _____

Words with *b*

1.

_____
_____ a t

2.

_____
_____ a t

3.

_____
m _____ n

4.

_____
c a _____

Directions Tell children to look at the first picture and help them name it. Then have them write the missing letter to complete the picture's name. Repeat with the rest of the pictures and words.

Have children circle the words with *b*. Say pairs of rhyming and non-rhyming words that go with each picture. Have children raise their hand when they hear a pair of words that rhyme.

Phonics

84

Kindergarten, Unit 3

Name _____

Cause and Effect

Cause

Effect

Directions Have children look at the picture and discuss what is happening. Then have them draw a picture of the effect it has in the **Big Book** selection. Have children share their pictures with the class and tell about the key event in their pictures. Then have them tell about another cause and effect that happens in *Turtle Splash!*

Comprehension

Kindergarten, Unit 3

Name _____

Action Verbs in the Past Tense

I   We

1. _____

2. _____

Directions Have children name each picture. Then have them complete each sentence by writing a word from the box and circling the picture that shows what happened in the past.

Have children read their sentences aloud using a past-tense verb to describe the picture they circled. Tell them to speak clearly as they share their sentences and to listen carefully to others as they share.

Name _____

| now | what | with | you |

1. _____ can you see?

2. I can see Pam _____ a bat.

3. _____ Pam can bat.

4. Bam! _____ can see Pam bat.

Directions Have children read the words in the box and look at each picture. Then have them write the correct word from the box to complete each sentence. Guide children to capitalize the first letter at the beginning of a sentence. Then have children read the sentences aloud. Have children point to and say the names of letters they recognize on the page. Then have them tap their desks once for each word as they read the sentences aloud again. Have children tell a story using all of the Words to Know.

Name _____

My Story

Directions Help children discuss and **generate ideas** for their own stories. Have children write ideas and draw pictures for their stories in the spaces in the graphic organizer. Guide children to write words or draw pictures showing the characters, setting, and what will happen in their stories.

Writing

Kindergarten, Unit 3

Name _____

1. Aa Aa Ff Ff Nn Nn Bb Bb

2.

  _____

  _____

  _____

  _____

  _____

  _____

Directions Have children write their name at the top of the page. Have them name each letter. Then have them trace *Aa*, *Ff*, *Nn*, and *Bb*.

Tell children to name the pictures and write the upper- and lowercase letters for the sound they hear at the beginning of each name. Remind children to write the letters so they can be easily read, using a left-to-right and top-to-bottom progression.

Phonics

89

Kindergarten, Unit 3

Name _____

My Story

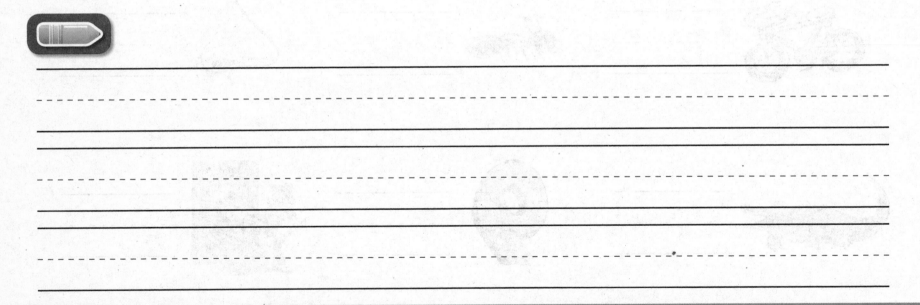

Directions Have children use pages 90–91 to draft, revise, and edit their story. Encourage children to use their ideas from **Reader's Notebook** page 88 as a guide in their writing. As children **develp their drafts**, remind them that they will have a chance to add to their story on another day. As children **revise** their drafts, discuss sentences and details they could add to make their story even better. As children **edit their drafts**, help them use what they know about letters and sounds to check the spelling of words. Have them check their sentences for correct capitalization and punctuation.

Writing

Kindergarten, Unit 3

Name _____

My Story

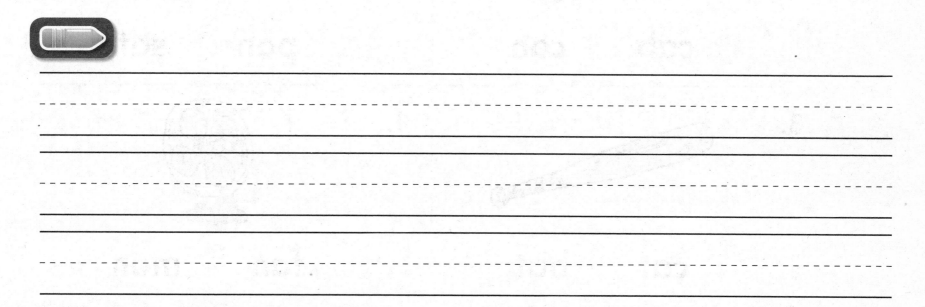

Directions Have children use pages 90–91 to draft, revise, and edit their story. Encourage children to use their ideas from **Reader's Notebook** page 88 as a guide in their writing. As children **develp their drafts**, remind them that they will have a chance to add to their story on another day. As children **revise their drafts**, discuss sentences and details they could add to make their story even better. As children **edit their drafts**, help them use what they know about letters and sounds to check the spelling of words. Have them check their sentences for correct capitalization and punctuation.

Name _____

Review Words with *a*, *n*, *f*, *b*

1.

cab   can

2.

pan   sat

3.

cat   bat

4.

fan   man

Directions Tell children to look at the first picture. Then have them circle the word that matches the picture. Repeat with the rest of the pictures and words.

Have children say the words that match each picture. Then have them think of words that rhyme with each one.

92

Sequence of Events

Directions Have children look at the pictures. Discuss what the author tells about at the beginning of the selection. Then have children draw a picture of something the author tells about at the end of the selection. Have children share their pictures.

Have them use sequence words, such as *first, next,* and *last,* to retell the selection in the order in which the author tells about things in the sky.

Comprehension

Kindergarten, Unit 3

Name _____

Statements

1. the moon and stars

2. we see an airplane

3. _____

4. _____

Then help children rewrite each statement correctly. Have them change the beginning letter of the first word to a capital letter and add a period to the end. Read the statements aloud with children.

Grammar

Kindergarten, Unit 3

a b c d e f g

h i j k l m n

o p q r s t

u v w x y z

A	A	A	B	B	C	C	D	D
E	E	E	F	F	G	G	H	H
I	I	J	J	K	K	L	L	M
M	N	N	O	O	P	P	Q	Q
R	R	S	S	T	T	U	U	V
V	W	W	X	X	Y	Y	Z	Z

d	d	c	c	b	b	a	a	a
h	h	g	g	f	f	e	e	e
m	l	l	k	k	j	j	i	i
q	q	p	p	o	o	n	n	m
v	u	u	t	t	s	s	r	r
z	z	y	y	x	x	w	w	v

see	I
we	like
a	the
to	and

you	come
what	me
are	with
now	my